First Flight

Other Books by Noriko and Don Carroll

Happy Birthday, the Cat

First Flight

A Mother Hummingbird's Story

Noriko and Don Carroll

**Andrews McMeel
Publishing, LLC**

Kansas City

09 10 TWP 10 9 8 7 6 5 4

ISBN-13: 978-0-7407-5707-5

ISBN-10: 0-7407-5707-5

Library of Congress Control Number: 2005932617

www.andrewsmcmeel.com

Designed by Desiree Mueller

*For Honey, who mesmerized and inspired us
to photograph and write this book.*

Contents

Acknowledgments

We would like to thank Judy Singer, who preserved Honey's nest and passed its care along to us. Our deep respect and thanks to our editor, Chris Schillig, for her great suggestions and skillful editing. We are also grateful to our agent, Al Zuckerman of Writers House, for his insightful advice and encouragement. Our special thanks to our friends, the Del Toro family, for always finding us new hummingbirds' nests to photograph and sharing the joy of watching them; John Klicka, curator of birds at the Marjorie Barrick Museum of Natural History, UNLV, for sharing his knowledge; Carolyn and Charles White, who gave us creative suggestions and encouraged us in so many ways; Marie and Brian Noonan, for helping us with research and spending long hours on our text; and all of our friends and family, for your support and patiently waiting for our backyard experience to become a book. We also would like to thank the National Audubon Society, the Hummingbird Society, the Arizona-Sonora Desert Museum, the Hilton Pond Center for Piedmont Natural History, and hummingbird banders and researchers, for their dedication, knowledge, and efforts to conserve hummingbirds and wildlife.

First Flight

Las Vegas

BE CAREFUL! HUMMINGBIRD'S NEST ABOVE!

We noticed the handwritten sign on a piece of cardboard the day we moved from New York City to our new house in Las Vegas, Nevada. Looking up, we saw a small nest on a clothesline between two wooden clothespins that stabilized it. A strong desert wind blew and tree branches swayed, but the small nest swung only slightly. Then, a hummingbird flew into it. Honey was the first neighbor to greet us.

Our suburban house, with its view of glittering casinos in the distance, is a desert oasis—for hummingbirds. An abundance of flowers is in bloom— honeysuckle, bird of paradise, primrose, aloe, salvia, sage, lavender, jasmine, and many other wildflowers and desert plants rich in nectar. Small insects swarm in a lush green backyard, and there are many old-growth trees on which hummers like to perch. The former owner had planted most of the garden to attract hummingbirds, and she had told us that Honey had been nesting on the clothesline for several years.

The Nest

As the scent of jasmine filled our back porch in the spring, Honey came back from her winter vacation in Mexico and hovered over her old nest. Showing no sign of fatigue from the long journey, she started working on it immediately. Although it had shrunk a little since last summer because of the dry air, it still held its shape, since it was protected from the elements by the roof. Honey fluffed the old fibers and brought new building materials—spider silk, downy plant fibers, lint, and small feathers—from our garden one beakful at a time. She bound these materials together using large amounts of spider web, wrapping it around the wooden clothespin, securing it to the nest, and stuffing the inside with

softer materials with her long bill and tongue. For about five days, she spent several hours each day renovating. The cozy little cup was almost ready for the arrival of her eggs.

While she was busy reconstructing, Don and I carefully set up a camera and flash units around Honey's nest. Our quiet back porch was converted into a delightful open-air photo studio. Each time new objects showed up around her nest, Honey cautiously approached and checked them out. She hovered, zigzagging to carefully examine a camera on a tripod, strobes, ladders, and mirrors. Often, she hovered right in front of us with her dark round eyes curiously watching.

Two Pearls

One April morning, Honey wiggled and shifted in the nest.

She lifted herself up, peered beneath her belly, then flew off to feed. We looked into the nest, and to our delight, there was a tiny white egg about the size of a jellybean. It was slightly translucent, almost glowing from within. Honey's first egg announced the arrival of spring.

Two days later, we carefully climbed the ladder to peek in and found two lovely, lustrous, elliptical-shaped pearls lying side by side. Precious. Pure. Perfect. They were so tiny, but quite large in proportion to Honey's small body. An energetic mom, she showed no fatigue from her days of labor and the delivery of two eggs. Now she spent all day and night on the nest incubating the eggs with only short breaks for feeding.

Honey rotated the tiny eggs with her feet, and we saw them pointing in different directions every time she left the nest. She fluffed her chest feathers and spread them over the eggs to keep them warm. Honey kept adding materials to the nest during incubation in an effort to maintain reliable warmth and maximize comfort for her future chicks. She curved the top edge of the nest inward to keep the eggs from accidentally rolling out during the high winds of spring.

Birthday Presents

After about two weeks of incubation, we noticed that the eggs had a slight discoloration. One morning, Honey stood on the rim staring into the nest, hovered above, then took off. A chick was pecking holes from inside the egg. The shell vibrated from the constant pecking, slowly broke open, and split in half. The first baby hummingbird emerged, and we named him Ray.

Quickly, Honey flew back. Ray instinctively threw his head back upon her arrival and opened his tiny yellow mouth. She sat on the edge of the nest carefully inspecting the new hatchling, then tenderly fed him his first meal of the sweet sustaining nectar. Welcome to the world, Ray!

Zen hatched early the next morning. This surprised and delighted us because it was also Noriko's birthday. These little wiggling birthday presents were so frail and helpless—they were blind and naked. A patch of blondish fuzzy natal down was still wet on their backs. Their semitransparent skins were wrinkled, dark brown on the back and pinkish on the belly. Bulbous and closed, their dark eyes took up most of their faces, which were made even more comical by their flat yellow beaks. These tiny creatures looked more like aliens than hummingbirds.

Honey picked up the shattered eggshells and tossed them from the nest. The shells were delicate, like fine Japanese rice paper, so it only took about thirty minutes to complete the hatching. This was very fast compared to the chicks of some larger birds that spend a couple of days breaking their hard eggshell.

Every fifteen to thirty minutes, Honey went off to hunt food for the chicks and herself. Born blind but hungry, the chicks must have heard or felt the air pressure from Honey's beating wings, since they raised their heads and pointed their yellow beaks up toward her when she returned and landed on the edge of the nest. They didn't chirp or fight over who got food first. Well behaved, these wriggling little raisins were always fed in turn, and we could almost see them growing by the hour.

Feeding time looked more like an assault than a tender moment. In our close-up photographs, we were astounded to see how deep Honey forced her beak into the newborn chicks' throats and stomachs, transferring food with a rapid up-and-down pumping motion of her head. When the chicks' small stomachs were full, they closed their mouths and slid back down into the nest to sleep. Honey sat on them, fluffing her chest and stomach feathers to blanket them because the blondish downy feathers on their backs were not enough to keep them warm.

Really Big Appetites

Hummingbirds may be among the world's smallest birds, but gram for gram of body weight, they are probably the biggest eaters. Because of their high metabolism, they have to consume several times their body weight in nectar and insects each day. Honey spent a lot of time foraging for the growing chicks who required more and more to eat every day. Hovering at one of the hummingbirds' favorite flowers, penstemon, she inserted her long translucent tongue, which was brushy at the tip, up into the flower, lapping it about thirteen times per second to glean nectar from inside the base of the flower.

Honey occasionally returned with yellow pollen dust on her head and beak. While hunting sweet nectar, she was pollinating each flower she visited. Honey brought Ray and Zen nature's supernutritional supplement. Pollen contains vitamins, proteins, minerals, amino acids, hormones, enzymes, and fats, but insects are the main source of protein and fats in a hummingbird's gourmet diet. From our garden, small flies, mosquitoes, gnats, moths, and spiders rounded out the menu. Honey plucked them from the air by positioning herself under them with her mouth open. One quick jump, and she could pop one into her mouth, then reposition herself and pop in another.

Honey often flew off beyond our garden, but when she came back, she always took a long drink—fifteen to thirty seconds—at our feeder before she went back to the nest. This was her feeder and her territory; these were her flowers, trees, and insects, and she relied on this bounty to raise her babies. Since hummingbirds are attracted to the color of the flower, not the color of nectar, we didn't color the sugar water in her feeder, mixing one part sugar to four parts water to simulate nectar.

The thin veil covering Ray and Zen's eyes split in about a week, and their curious eyes looked out at this world full of mystery. Their heads popped up like two hungry jacks-in-the-box when Honey landed on the edge of the nest with her crop (storage pouch) full of nutritious mixtures. She seemed to divide the meal equally between the two, taking turns going back and forth. As they grew, they were more and more eager to eat Honey's gourmet food, stretching their necks to meet her bill. The small world of the hummingbird nest seemed peaceful, and we didn't observe any sibling rivalry between Ray and Zen.

The hummingbird chicks instinctively kept the inside of the nest free from feces. We observed their targeted missile launches after the first days of feeding, but occasionally the trajectory fell short and their waste landed on the edge of the nest. The babies couldn't get it right every time!

Flight Secret

We marveled at the precision and grace of Honey's flight. Hummingbirds can reach speeds of up to 60 mph, freely changing direction and stopping instantaneously to hover in midair. Not only can they fly backward, they can also fly upside down for brief periods. Honey entertained us every day by zipping through our garden and into the porch, hovering like a fairy in the air. Like a magician, she disappeared and then reappeared instantly before our eyes.

The maneuverability of a hummingbird's flight would make the designer of the most advanced military helicopters envious. A hummingbird's wings are unique among birds, and their flight is similar to that of an insect. The wing's bone structure is like a human arm with fused elbow and wrist joints. They rotate and pivot at the shoulders. When Honey hovered, she moved her fully extended wings forward and backward while pivoting the leading edge of the wing, thereby tracing a figure eight pattern parallel to the ground. She used her tail feathers as a rudder, allowing her to maintain any body position. A hummingbird's normal wing beat is about fifty to seventy times per second. During courtship flight, the male's wing can beat two hundred times per second, resulting in a high-pitched hum.

At ten and eleven days of age, Ray and Zen looked like miniature porcupines. Honey no longer sat on the chicks. They could maintain their own body temperatures of 106 degrees Fahrenheit. Their plumage was in the earliest stage of development, and they still had some fuzzy, blond natal feathers on their backs that disappeared as they grew. Ray proudly showed his wings, stretching them in the warm air. They were covered with the quills that would become his flight feathers. Zen's beak peeked out from under Ray's wing like a periscope. Its tip was starting to turn from baby yellow to juvenile brown, rapidly elongating. Within a few short weeks, the chicks' wings would be developed enough to fly, but first they needed fuller feathers and a lot of flapping practice.

At age two weeks, Ray and
Zen started to flap their developing
wings when they were not sleeping
or eating. Their immature flight
feathers now looked like tiny
artist's brushes hanging from their
wing tips. Ray spread his wings,
lightly stretched, and moved them

a few times in the air, as if he was shaking imaginary paint from his brushes. Then he quickly folded them back into the nest. Zen immediately followed, imitating Ray. This was their first attempt at exercising their growing wings—Flying Lesson One.

43

In Lesson Two, they stretched their bodies upward, beating the air with flapping wings. With each movement, they were gaining muscle mass, just as we humans do when we exercise. They need to develop strong flight muscles to become the lightweight champions of flight.

Practice, Practice

Ray and Zen yearned for flight. Their eyes followed Honey flying out to the world beyond the porch, and their heads turned in the direction of her flight as if synchronized. She took off from the nest almost instantaneously, and she could reach top speed in as few as three wing beats—an incomprehensibly short amount of time! Excited, Ray and Zen became more active immediately after Honey flew away. They frantically flapped their wings and preened themselves. The small nest was not a sleepy town anymore.

When one started to flap, the other had to duck for cover. As they climbed onto the edge, grabbing firmly with their sharp toenails, they stretched their necks, pointed their elongated orange beaks forward, and flapped their wings, simulating flight. They moved their wings as fast as they could and would have lifted off if they lost their long-toed, tight grip on the edge of the nest.

Soon Ray and Zen began to struggle for comfort and space. The nest was quite elastic and continued to stretch as they grew. Still, two became a crowd. Sometimes one baby climbed on the other's back, slipping and sliding while enthusiastically flapping its wings. At times they practiced simultaneously with one losing its balance and almost falling off the edge, but recovering equilibrium just in time.

Honey no longer fed the chicks by perching on the nest. Instead, she began aerial refueling, hovering above because Ray and Zen's feathers had overflowed the edges of the nest.

Preening

High-performance flight requires hummingbirds to meticulously maintain their wings, and preening is essential to conditioning the feathers. Honey never preened on the nest in front of the chicks, so it must be instinctive behavior since they started preening as soon as their wings emerged. Honey perched on a twig, ruffled the feathers on her head and body—the perfect model for a bad hair day. She scratched her head with one foot while standing on the other with perfect balance, pointing her bill straight up in the air as if she was performing an exotic dance. During a passing thunderstorm, she joyously caught raindrops on her feathers while perched.

Ray and Zen performed this same procedure together in the small nest in between flight training sessions. They seemed to scratch their bodies more frequently than Honey did when preening, as if emerging new feathers were tickling them. They were not only scratching, however, but also removing dirt and parasites from their bodies and plumage by nibbling at them with their rapidly elongating bills and combing through their feathers with their toenails. During preening, Ray and Zen also applied waterproofing oil to their feathers from a small, pimple-sized gland located on their lower backs at the base of their tail feathers.

Who's Who

We were very curious about what species Honey belonged to, and we watched her and her young at every possible opportunity, trying to gather information to identify them, but females and young hummingbirds are difficult to distinguish in some species. We watched for the more easily recognizable males, but for a long time there were none around to give us clues to Honey's identity because male hummers don't participate in nesting activity.

Who is Honey? This simple question remained a mystery until we observed Honey engaged in a dazzling courtship flight with a male Black-chinned whom we nicknamed Bluebeard. He was slightly smaller than Honey's three and a half-inch length, and his head and face were velvety black with an elegant band of iridescent purple on the gorget bordering his white chest. The purple band appeared black most of the time, but when the light struck the feathers directly, they sparkled like precious sapphires. Over a blooming white oleander tree against the clear blue sky, Bluebeard performed an aeronautical show, flying to a height of about twenty-five feet and making several U-shaped dive displays. Each time he approached the bottom of the U, he produced a lovely flute-like sound. Then he flew a jerky, side-to-side shuttle motion accompanied by a distinct, high-pitched buzz. He momentarily disappeared, then suddenly, both he and Honey darted out from the oleander, and she zoomed back to our porch. Hummingbirds are promiscuous, so we don't know for sure that energetic, handsome Bluebeard is Ray and Zen's dad. But their courtship helped us finally identify Honey as a Black-chinned Hummingbird, and this was confirmed by John Klicka, curator of birds at the Marjorie Barrick Museum of Natural History at the University of Nevada–Las Vegas. He positively identified Honey from our photographs and explained that the spotting we had observed on her throat is characteristic of a female Black-chin.

A Guardian Angel

One morning, our cat, Birthday, was lazing on an antique iron chair on the porch, and the morning sun enveloped her from behind, highlighting her beautiful fur. Suddenly, Honey appeared hovering six inches above Birthday's head. Her wings were as luminescent as an angel's. The scene looked so peaceful, like the Garden of Eden. Then Honey started buzzing aggressively over Birthday's fuzzy ears to chase her away from her territory. Honey normally kept a wise distance from our cats, observing them quietly. However, she was deliberately provoking the sleepy giant this morning. We knew the time must be getting very close for the babies to fly, and so the young hummers were very vulnerable to predators.

Parting Gestures

Next morning, Don furiously chased Birthday into the house, ears flattened to her head, as he scolded, "Birthday, you are bad!" He quickly explained that Honey had dive-bombed Birthday with her sharp beak. Surprised, Birthday tried to defend herself—she swatted at Honey but missed. While we scolded the wrongfully accused victim, through the open door we saw Ray slowly lift himself up above the nest! He looked wobbly, as if in a slow-motion movie. We were so excited we nearly missed the shot. Luckily, Don hit the remote button twice and captured the moment of Ray's departure, flapping his matured wings proudly with his feet kicking air.

Alone in the nest,
Zen stared up in wonder
as tiny droplets of Ray's
urine fell from above.
Ray flew successfully
out of the roofed porch
and landed safely on a
nearby chinaberry tree.
Honey flew to his side
immediately to celebrate
his departure and fed him.

71

A fledged young hummingbird makes high-pitched chirping sounds that enable the mother to locate it. Ray and Zen never chirped in the nest until Ray's departure. Left alone, Zen chirped and sounded insecure, more lonely than hungry. She stood on the nest rim and frantically flapped her wings, trying to lift herself up in the air. Zen chirped loudly to let Honey know she was still there and perhaps communicate with Ray on the tree. We heard both Ray and Zen chirping back and forth. Honey was even busier flying between the nest and the tree feeding the now separated young chicks. Ray was elated and excited. He investigated everything he came across—leaves, nuts, bees, and butterflies. He made short flights between the branches, perfecting his flight techniques, and preened his new wings constantly. Ray stayed in the same tree all day, and we followed him with a camera and ladder.

The next morning, Zen waited for no one but took off at dawn before we awoke. We immediately searched for her, but she let us know where she was with her little squeaky voice. She had landed on a shaggy palm leaf about eight feet from the nest but only a couple of feet from the ground—a vulnerable place for a baby hummer. She looked at us nervously from between layers of scraggy green leaves. Although she tried to hold onto the palm leaf with her small feet, she continually slid down, flapping her wings to maintain balance, her little toes curled insecurely around the slick palm fibers. She chirped loudly for help, but we could do nothing except take photographs and cheer her on.

Suddenly Zen flew unsteadily with desperate wing flaps and landed on the spiked palm stem, struggling to gain her balance. She sat timidly between the spikes that looked like shark's teeth, making her seem all the more vulnerable. Once more she took flight, but again, she landed on another unstable palm leaf. Her little squeaky voice got louder. Poor little Zen was having a much rougher departure than Ray.

Attentive mom that she was, Honey chattered lightly as she hovered over Zen, encouraging her to fly. Excited, Zen chirped and flapped her new wings frantically. Honey hovered trying to feed her, but Zen kept sliding down the leaf. A quick beak-to-beak feeding was not enough, but Honey could only stay near and watch. Zen pointed her beak high, propelling her wings determinedly. Slowly she lifted herself out of the shaggy palm and landed securely in the jasmine vines where clusters of small white flowers fragrantly greeted the morning sun—a much safer place for a novice wing flapper.

Good morning, Zen! For the first time, she could relax after leaving the nest. Zen preened her wings and scratched her head and neck with her short feet, looking like a dancer on a tightrope. Honey joined her and happily fed her a big reward.

While Zen stayed in the jasmine
performing her dancing act, Ray flew back
to the porch and hovered over Don's camera.
He landed on the lens and peered into it for
an extreme close-up. Then he flew up to the
remote receiver mounted on top of the camera
and struck a pose. Curiosity had finally gotten
the better of him.

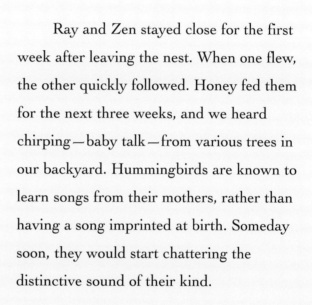

Ray and Zen stayed close for the first week after leaving the nest. When one flew, the other quickly followed. Honey fed them for the next three weeks, and we heard chirping—baby talk—from various trees in our backyard. Hummingbirds are known to learn songs from their mothers, rather than having a song imprinted at birth. Someday soon, they would start chattering the distinctive sound of their kind.

The young hummingbirds' education had begun. Ray and Zen inspected everything with great interest, learning which flowers were worth visiting, where the feeders were, and how to protect themselves from predators. They were learning about their new territory. How do they know when to migrate south, we wondered? We didn't know for sure if Ray was male or Zen was female, but in our hearts that's whom they would always be.

Tree Nests

About a week after Ray and Zen fledged, our neighbor told us that he had found another hummingbird's nest in a fruitless mulberry tree in his yard. The nest was newly made under a protective four-inch leaf for shade and camouflage, and it was situated in the fork of a branch about the thickness of a pencil. We discovered four other incomplete nests in nearby trees and climbed a ladder to peek into the finished nest while Honey sat on a branch and observed. There was one egg in the nest, and a second was laid the following day. Honey flew back and forth from the feeder on our back porch to the tree nest next door, a distance of about sixty feet. Ray and Zen often perched in the mulberry or the oleander. Honey was incubating the new eggs while still continuing to feed them. Talk about multitasking!

The two eggs hatched, but only one chick survived to maturity in the extremely hot, dry weather throughout June. By the time Ray and Zen's new sibling had fledged, it was impossible to tell who was who anymore. There were many more hummingbirds with some or no coloring showing up at our feeder in June and July, and we suspected many of them were juveniles newly fledged in the neighborhood.

We know of at least eight baby hummingbirds that Honey raised in the three years since that first nest we observed, sometimes nurturing more than one clutch of youngsters in a season.

Every year, we learned more and more about the hummingbirds in our backyard. We've found Costa's Hummingbirds wintering here, and we discovered a nest built on a pinecone high up in one of our trees in January. Two chicks fledged in early March and were soon buzzing around the yard. Then in April, to our delight, Honey came back and and started remodeling her old nest on the clothesline.

Now, when a hummer hovers over our heads or sits chattering on a branch near us, we wonder and often ask, "Are you Honey's baby?"

Photographic Notes

Honey gave us an amazing opportunity to document her nesting activity. An open view of the nest with 360-degree access allowed us to set up cameras and lights as we wanted. All the photographs were captured with digital cameras. When Ray and Zen were still small and hidden in the bottom of the nest, we used a mirror and photographed the reflection instead of mounting the heavy camera over the nest. The mirror was the kind used in scientific experiments; the silver coating was on the front surface of the glass, so that it gave a perfect reflection without the ghost effect and green cast. We also often used another mirror to reflect various areas of our flower garden for a variety of backgrounds that created a pleasing natural light behind the nest. This multiple-exposure shot shows the pivoting body movement of a male Black-chin. We love to experiment with photography.